No Childhood

By

Edith Rogers

ISBN: 1-4033-8931-4 (e-book)
ISBN: 1-4033-8932-2 (Paperback)

This book is printed on acid free paper.

1stBooks - rev. 11/18/02

It's been a long time since the start and end of the holocaust. A lot has been written about that time, the horror it wrought, the lives it destroyed. Movies, stage plays, memoirs of survivors are many. So why another one?

For a long time I felt that it was over, nothing could be changed and dwelling on it was only harmful to one's health. But now, that I am in the senior years of my life, I feel that I need to let everyone in my family know what made me the person I am.

So this little book is dedicated to my children, grandchildren, great grandchildren, and future ones yet to come.

It is also a tribute to my mother and little brother who perished in Auschwitz, along with millions of others.

Let it also be a thank you for the wonderful people who went to great length to keep me safe. And let it serve as a reminder, that even in a place where good people live, evil can dominate.

Don't let it happen again...

The following remembrances of the Holocaust and World War II are dedicated to Dad, Mom and the girls. And to the Sisters, the teachers, the ministers, neighbors and the many others who helped protect me and other children from certain torture and death.

They are also dedicated to Mutti, Peter and the six million Jews and six million other victims of the Nazis.

But most of all, to my children, grandchildren, great grand children and the generations after them, so they will not forget what happened, and thus make sure history does not repeat itself.

I also want to thank everyone who encouraged me to write this account, because I needed their support.

And I need to say that I am glad Dad was right and I did come to America and become a proud citizen of the greatest place on earth.

WHAT CHILD?

I HEAR YOU SAY "WHEN I WAS A CHILD IN THE GOOD OLD DAYS"

SO I THINK BACK AND TRY TO FIND,

WHEN I WAS A CHILD, AT LEAST IN MY MIND.

TRY AS I MIGHT, I CANNOT SEE

THE LONG AGO LITTLE GIRL THAT SHOULD HAVE BEEN ME.

THEY TOOK IT FROM ME, MY CHILDHOOD…

Edith Rogers

IT WAS GONE, BEFORE MY LIFE HAD BARELY BEGUN.

PLEASE PUT ME DOWN

JUST BECAUSE FIRES ARE BURNING ALL OVER
TOWN

YOU ARE CARRYING ME LIKE A BABY, PLEASE
PUT ME DOWN.

WHY WON'T YOU LET ME WALK ON MY OWN?

A LOT OF STORE WINDOWS AND THE TEMPLES
ARE SHATTERED.

YOU HAVE TEARS IN YOUR EYES, YOU KEEP
SHAKING YOUR HEAD.

BUT TO ME, NONE OF THAT REALLY MATTERED.

I AM NOT A BABY,

PLEASE PUT ME DOWN.

WHY WON'T YOU LET ME WALK ON MY OWN?

YOU TELL ME I MUST NEVER FORGET

WHAT I AM SEEING HERE TONIGHT.

I MUST BE PROUD OF MY HERITAGE,

NO MATTER THE 'OTHERS' POWER AND MIGHT.

THAT IT IS A HORRIBLE THING THE NAZIS ARE DOING.

SURELY THEIR DAY OF RECKONING WILL BE FORTHCOMING.

YOU HAVE TALKED LIKE THIS BEFORE AND I REALLY DO LISTEN.

AND YET, WHAT IF MY FRIENDS ARE AROUND?

THEY'LL THINK I AM A BABY, PLEASE PUT ME DOWN.

WHY WON'T YOU LET ME WALK ON MY OWN?

THE YEARS HAVE GONE BY, SOME MEMORIES FADE.

BROKEN GLASS AND FIRES STILL GENERATE

A CERTAIN FEAR AND HORROR IN MY SOUL.

IT TOOK SO MANY LIFETIMES FOR ME TO UNDERSTAND,

BY CARRYING ME IN YOUR ARMS AND HAND

YOU SAVED MY LIFE THAT VERY NIGHT, SO LONG AGO.

AND MANY OTHER TIMES TOO, I NOW KNOW.

IT IS FAR TOO LATE TO TELL YOU HOW GRATEFUL I AM

THAT YOU NEVER LISTENED TO MY MOAN AND GROAN.

I COULD NOT HAVE WALKED THROUGH THE HOLOCAUST ALONE.

THANK GOD, YOU DID NOT PUT ME DOWN.

Edith Rogers

AIR RAID AT THE PARK

Last night was a bad raid. When we walked down to the park this morning, we found a real bad scene. There were pieces of lady-soldiers all over the place. In trees and bushes and on the ground. Seems a bomb hit right in the middle of a unit of women soldiers on their way to the train station. (the park is a short cut to the Bahnhof (train depot) and we all take it all the time. But I guess the ladies did not have time to get to a shelter, before the bombs hit. Dad says it hit right in the middle of them. Marion threw up when she saw it, because her big sister is a soldier and I guess she thought it could have been her.

We also find out that Trudy, Irma's friend, who was gonna have a baby, died in the air raid last night. She was on the way to a shelter, but didn't make it. It was one of those where we did not get warned and it was too late. I don't want to go to the funeral. I hate them. But Dad says we have to show our respect to Trudy's parents, especially since her husband is in the war and cannot be there.

AIRRAID WARDEN

I am now an official air raid warden. I am 12 years old. I have a uniform, a helmet and an armband. Whenever there is an alarm or airraid, I have to make sure that everyone on my block is off the street and in the cellar. I have to make sure there are no lights on anywhere. And I have to make sure that Mrs. G. next door has the two babies in the baskets and help her take them to the cellar. They are 6 months old and two years old. And then after the airraid and the all clear I have to go thru the building and make sure there are no fires.

Frau H. does not like this, she does not think you can trust a dirty Jew to go through the building without them stealing you blind. But when Dad suggested that one of her boys could go with me, she backed off fast. Guess she thinks whatever makes me a Jew might rub off on them or something.

Dad says don't pay any attention, but I do get upset about it.

Mom is very angry. She says they won't let me in school, they will not give me food coupons, but I have to be an air raid warden. Dad says it might help to get them off my back for awhile. Don't know what that means, but he is so smart, he is probably right.

CATTLECARS...

When you see a cattle car go past at a railroad crossing, what do you really see?

Do you ever wonder who or what may be riding inside? Of course not! Anyone knows that there are animals inside. Animals such as cows, pigs, goats etc. Except in Germany during WWII. The Nazis have a different idea of what animals are. They consider Jews, Gypsies, Mentally or Physically Handicapped, Politically Incorrect and anyone else who is not PURE ARIAN, which means blond, blue-eyed and German to the Nth generation back, as animals. So, that means they should be put into cattle cars. And let's stack them up. Hundreds to each car. Then transport them to places like Dachau, Theresienstadt, Bergen, and others. After all, we build these places for animals like them.

The sign at the entrance says"Arbeit macht Frei" which means 'work brings freedom'.

For many of the thousands per train, which survived the trip, without food or water, and lack of air, sanitary accommodations, or places to put the ones who did not survive, the slogan at the entrance actually came true. They were worked to death, tortured, and murdered. To most of them, death did mean freedom.

As hundreds and thousands of trains of cattle cars made their way across Europe and Germany, many people stood at the side of the road or at the crossings and watched the trains go by. Many jeered, laughed, whistled, threw insults and often rocks at the cars. Others turned discreetly away, able to always maintain their innocence by not seeing "anything". But there were others. People who openly cried, cursed the Nazis at their own risk. And some pushed apples, a piece of bread, a boiled potato through the bars. They knew the chances they were taking. They knew they would get killed if they were caught, but they did it anyway. Those were the Germans no one talked about after the war. But they are remembered by the few survivors who returned.

I remember being taken to one of the cattle cars coming through town. Father told me that Mutti and Peter were on the train. I do not remember whether I actually saw anyone I remember the screams I heard. And the moaning and the horrible smells. To this day, there are times when I am at a railroad crossing and I hear a calf or a pig inside a car, I am taken back in time to the sounds and smells of that day.

When I went to the Holocaust Museum in D. C., I was able to keep from getting upset at what I saw... until I stepped on the cattle car sitting in the middle of one of the floors. I started shaking and crying and actually got physically ill.

I tried to think of the people who survived, the people who tried to help. But all I could think of was my mother and brother and the millions of others, who spent days and weeks in a car like this. It is impossible to fathom what they went through and no one will ever be able to explain it.

THERESIENSTADT...

I got a card from Mutti to-day. It came from Theresienstadt. She says both she and Peter are fine. And I can write to her and send her a picture and packages. I have to send them to some address in Berlin. But Theresienstadt is nowhere near Berlin. I know, because I looked it up. Took a long time to find too. And why is she now Ilse Sarah Salomon? Her name is Ilse Liselotte Trzeciak, nee Salomon. I do not understand this.

When I ask, I am told 'It's the Law'. Sounds stupid to me. That night I heard Dad tell Mom that Ilse is never coming back. He is crying and telling Mom he should not have stopped her from turning on the oven that night. I have no idea what he is talking about and if I ask the next morning, he will know I eavesdropped. (Have been doing a lot of that lately, since no one tells me what is going on because I am too young. What a joke, I am older than they think..) Anyway, years pass before I have the courage to ask Dad about his remarks to Mom. By then, Mutti and Peter are long presumed dead.

The story is this: Mutti called Dad one night to tell him she is going to kill herself and Peter. She is going to turn the gas on and they will go to sleep and won't have to worry about the Nazis coming to get them. Dad spent hours talking her out of it, a decision that haunted him until the day he died. No one else ever blamed him. No one knew what the future held for the Jews and other "undesirables". But Dad always carried that night with him. He was not a Jew, but he was a victim of the Holocaust just the same. It cost him his peace of mind long before he died. It is almost ironic, that Mutti and Peter almost certainly died by gas, albeit after other tortures and not by going to sleep.

17

Edith Rogers

COMING BACK

Dad took me to the train station to-day. Some trains are coming from the East with survivors of concentration camps. From what we have heard, concentration camps were places like Theresienstadt and Auschwitz and Dachau, and some others I have never heard of. Rumors are that a lot of people were tortured and mistreated there. (Of course, it was not until much later that we found out about the horror of the Holocaust and that whatever I and others like me suffered, was NOTHING compared to what went on.) Anyway, the people getting off the train looked awful. Like they were just skeletons. Dad was crying as we went from car to car. Of course we did not find Mutti. There were no children on the train so we knew Peter was not here.

After we went back home, Dad was telling Mom and the girls about it and they all cried. I did not, because I didn't know any of these people and Mutti had never looked like that. I do remember what she looks like.

Dad and I went to some more of the trains looking for Mutti and Peter. We never did find them, but some awfully skinny old woman said she knew Mutti and Peter in Theresienstadt and that they had been sent to Auschwitz. By then we had heard that noone from Auschwitz came back and Dad decided we would not go to any more trains. Instead he put some ads in the papers with pictures of Mutti and Peter, but noone ever answered. (In 1999 the Red Cross finally found out the numbers and dates of the transports that took them to Theresienstadt and later to Auschwitz. There the trail ends and we never did find the date of death or how they were killed.)

CRAZY EIGHT

Today Irma and I went to the country. We took some of Mom's linen and some nice clothes to trade for food. It's against the law, but who cares. Noone in my family likes any of the laws any longer.

Anyway, we got on our bikes and started out. When we got past the suburbs, we were in farm country. People were in the fields working. And Irma and I stopped to talk with them. I kind of wandered off to look around since I had never been in a field on a farm before.

All of a sudden a bunch of planes came over. They came real low and started shooting at us. Irma threw me in the ditch and herself on top of me. The planes went over three times and you could see the star on their wings. Irma says one person is dead and she helped the three who were hurt. Everyone screamed nasty words about Americans and English attacking poor farmers. I couldn't figure out why this was happening. After all, Dad had told me how decent and good Americans were. So why would they do this?

We did not do any trading that day and just went home as fast as we could. When we told Dad he said "Those are Nazi planes with false markings to make people hate the Allies. There is no way small Allied planes could come this far in the daylight without being shot down." He told us he had heard of this happening before. He told us it was usually eight planes and they called them the crazy eight. Is it possible that the Nazis are actually attacking their own farmers to make them hate someone? I mean, those farmers are not Jews. And Dad told us not to go trading anymore. But we will anyway, everyone is hungry and we can get some good stuff like eggs and meat.

ENGLISH

After I got kicked out of school, Dad hired that awful man down the street. He used to be a professor at an university, but he got fired because he would not join the party(whatever that means). So now I have him as my own private teacher. Dad says I must study every day, even a few hours on Sunday, so when the war is over I will be better educated and smarter than any of the other kids. I don't mind it much, except the professor is so mean. If I make one little mistake, he makes me do everything all over again. He even tells me things about history that are illegal. Of course, Dad made me swear on the Bible, before we even started, that I won't tell. Prof even tells me a few things about Jews, and he does not think we are all evil and dirty and smelly. Anyway, Dad says that I am now up to the first year of university knowledge, even if I am only 13.

I have been studying English out of a book, and Dad checks those assignments, since Prof does not speak English. I am getting real good too. Last night Dad and I listened on his funny type radio. It's a gas radio. Mom and the girls stayed near the door and the windows, in case someone would come. It is a big crime, and we would all get shot if we got caught listening to an English station or the Voice of America from a Swiss station. Anyway, I understood a lot of what they were saying. Of course I don't believe that they are coming soon, and that they are going to win the war. But Dad does and it makes him happy. I think we are all going to be dead before the English or Americans get here. Dad tells me to keep up with my studies, especially the English, because someday I will be going to America. Yeah, sure I will. And the Nazis will let me go. Right? But Dad says the war will be over soon. And everything will be ok. He even says Mutti will be home with Peter, and I know that is not true because I heard him tell Mom that Mutti is dead. But I just say that's great. I would never let him know that I stopped believing he can keep me safe a long time ago.

EXPLOSION

This has been a real bad day. Joseph is dead, and all of us kids in the group are to blame. You see, one of the real big deals, right now, is who has the best and largest splinter collection. A splinter collection is pieces of anti air craft bullets, and pieces of fire bombs dropped by the Allies. And everybody goes out and tries to get as many and as soon after a bombing as possible. Dad has told me a million times, and I think the other parents have told their kids too, not to touch any of that stuff. But who listens?

Anyway, the air raid last night did not do too much damage in our neighborhood, so all of the kids headed for the park this morning. One of the bigger boys, and I don't know which one, no matter how many times Dad asks me, found a fire bomb which did not go off. So he tossed it at a tree. Joseph was standing next to the tree and the thing exploded. Those firebombs only start fires, they do not explode. But this one did. Joseph was torn to pieces. Erik got a piece of something in his arm, but he is ok. I ran all the way home to get Dad, but nothing can be done. All the parents say it was an awful accident, and noone says it was our fault. But we all know they are thinking it. I know Frau H is going to blame me, even though the twins were there too. But then she always blames everything on me, including the war. It's because I am Jewish.

GUIDO

They took Guido away to-day. He is three years older than me. So he is 13. Dad says they came real early in the morning before anyone was up. It was the Gestapo and his grandmother couldn't do anything about it. His Mom and Dad and sister have been gone a long time and nobody knows where they are. Maybe they took him to his family. That would be nice.

So that leaves only three of us when we have to go to the Sisters. Esther, Miriam and me. No one knows what happened to Erika. She was just gone one day with her Mom and both her aunts. Dad says maybe they got away, but I don't think he believes it. So Mom keeps walking around with a long face all day. I see her cry a lot even when she tries to hide it. Is it my fault? If I wasn't here they would not have these problems and I heard some of the neighbors saying so. Mrs. H said they shouldn't be stuck with a dirty Jewish girl... again with the "dirty". I hate that woman. Sometimes I want to run away so they wouldn't be stuck with me. But where would I go? Nobody wants me except for Mom and Dad. They keep telling me it will all be ok soon and not to worry. But actually I don't believe it any more. Sooner or later the Gestapo will come and get me. I don't actually know what that means either, except that nobody ever comes back and I am so scared. I do know it is something really bad and everyone only talks in whispers about it.

LUTHERAN MINISTER

When I turned 12, Dad took me to see the Lutheran minister. He asked that he confirm me, and maybe that way the Nazis would leave me alone. Fat chance.. I was already sprinkled with Holy Water by a Catholic priest, and they still kicked me out of school. So I knew it wouldn't work. But I went along with it, especially since I was paired up with Fritz, whom I really liked, and his parents let him hang around with me. And I also got a new suit, shoes with little heels, that Mom had traded some silverware for. And some of the neighbors who liked Mom and Dad got together and baked some kind of a cake with real flour, not just potatoes.

There was a day raid on the Sunday morning that we were confirmed. It was done at an old school which was now an army hospital, because the church was already bombed out. Nobody, and I mean nobody, that was there went to the shelter, when the noise started. Fritz and I were confirmed as were the other kids and everyone sang songs, even with all the noise. Especially the soldiers in the wheelchairs. The minister said that God was with us and that was why nothing hit the school.

Well, that was about 6 months ago, and he was wrong. Because two days ago he was killed in an airraid. I have been asked by the other kids that were confirmed if I would say a poem and lay down a wreath at the funeral. I didn't want to, but Dad said I should. So ok, I went this afternoon. I had the wreath with little yellow roses in my hand, and I knew which poem I would read. Everything was fine until they brought the casket. Dad did not tell me that they only had one about the size of a cigar box, because they only found a jaw bone and a button from his cassock. I threw the wreath down and went screaming from the cemetery. Dad caught me down the street but I could not stop screaming. So he took me to Dr. Dora, and she gave me something to swallow. I think it was poison, but I stopped screaming and went to sleep for a while. I will never, ever go to another funeral as long as I live.

MANFRED

Dad has this apprentice. He is 14 or 15. I think he is the best looking boy I have ever seen. He is real nice to me, but only because of Dad. I bet he already has a girl friend.

Manfred wears his HitlerYouth uniform when he is not working with Dad. Bet if he knew I was Jewish he wouldn't be so nice to me. Once in a while he comes home with Dad and stays for supper. And we play cards or chess. I beat him at chess all the time, because I have been playing for a long time and he is just learning.

Manfred killed himself yesterday. Why would he do that?? I am devastated and Dad will not tell me why he did it. He wouldn't even tell me about it, but I heard the neighbors talking about it. I begged Dad to tell me, but he says I am too young. Always with the "too young". Doesn't anyone understand that kids like me are not young??

Well, I finally found out the whole story. Dad will be very angry if he knows I eavesdropped again. But how else am I supposed to know what is going on.?

Manfred's HitlerYouth group went to the woods a couple of weeks ago with some old Jewish men. They had to tell the men to dig graves. Then they had to shoot them and bury them in those graves. Well, Manfred's best friend, whom I do not know, wouldn't do it. So the group leader shot Manfred's best friend right in front of the group. It made all the rest of the group do what they were told. They were scared and did shoot the old Jewish men and then buried them. Manfred had told Dad all about it. And I guess he cried and cried and finally felt so bad that he went and shot himself. He shouldn't have done that, because it will not bring those Jewish men back and now Manfred's family and friends are very sad. I wish all this stuff would go away. Dad keeps telling me everything will be all right soon, but I do not believe him anymore. It's not that I think he is a liar. I think he keeps saying that so I won't be scared.

But I am scared all the time now.

MR. HAUG

They took Mr. Haug away during the night. I do not understand this. He is not Jewish, so why would they come for him? He is the teacher who put some wrong stuff in my record and a couple of other kids' records so we could still go to school. But the Nazis found out and we were kicked out of school anyway. The neighbors say that is why they came and took him away. I sure hope he comes back soon and does not get into any real trouble. Dad is telling me to pray for Mr. Haug. That is a bad sign and I think whatever happens is going to be my fault, since I am one of the kids the neighbors are talking about.

Mr. Haug never did come back and no one ever found out what happened to him. Does this make me guilty for him being gone or dead or whatever?

MUTTI

Mutti is no longer in Theresienstadt. Dad found out from one of his friends at the Gauamt... city hall.

She was transferred to the East, whatever that means. Dad says we have to pray a lot for her and Peter.

That does not sound very good to me. I will do it, but only to make Dad happy. I really don't believe it will do any good. Dad says everything will be fine, but I know he is only saying that to make me feel better. If everything is going to be ok, why are Mom and the girls always crying, when they think I can't see it? They all know something I don.t. Wonder what it is...

AIRRAIDS (AT HOME AND AT THE SISTERS)

We had another real bad one last night, but I wasn't really scared. Dad and I stayed on the veranda as long as we could. We enjoyed watching the Christmas trees coming down... actually they are flares to light up the targets... but they are colorful and as long as you don't think about their real reason, well, anyway.

When the bombs started falling, we ran for the cellar. When we finally came back up, I don't know how long we were in the cellar, everything on the block was burning. Our building was the only one still standing. We have no windows. Most of the furniture is tipped over. Mom is crying and carrying on over some broken dishes and canned fruit in glass jars.

I am really scared because everything in the neighborhood is destroyed and we have some fires in the building too. But I cannot tell anyone, because I have to go to the Apotheke (pharmacy) and help. Everyone is still trapped under the rubble and we can hear the signal, so we know they are alive and we have to get them out. We can also hear that big dog howling. It belongs to the pharmacist and his wife and I am real afraid of that dog. And he sounds so eerie under the rubble.

It's three hours later. We hear no more signals and even the dog only yelps a little every now and then. So we stop digging. All the adults in our group are crying. We, the other kids and me, are just glad we are getting a break. The pharmacist and his wife are, I mean, were nice people. The Russian prisoners will dig their bodies out to-morrow. And I don't really care that much. Two of my friends, and I only have a few anyway, got killed in airraids last week. And maybe to-night will be our turn. Sometimes *I* think maybe that wouldn't be so bad. At least, we wouldn't be so scared all the time. Dad asked me if I am ok. And there I go, screaming, shaking, crying like a baby. I am almost 11 years old, and carrying on like a baby. What is wrong with me? I am not afraid of airraids, and bombs, and digging out people. Why am I acting like this. Dad slapped me... He never hits me. Why is he so mad at me? Well, I'll show him I am no baby. I stop crying and run in the building.

AT THE SISTERS

From the minute the shooting alarm goes off, I am awfully scared. Dad isn't here to protect me. The sisters take me and the others in their basement. They don't have a cellar. And we can't go to the priest's house, since he doesn't know about us.

The sisters are down on their knees and praying with those pearls they use for prayer. The are called rosaries, I think. We can hear the bombs and we cry for them to stop. Will anyone in our family still be alive? What if they are bombed out and have to leave for somewhere else without us? Will we ever find them or see them again? What if the Nazis finds us and our families won't know where we are?

Sister Elfriede, my favorite, promises she will go tomorrow and find out for us. But what if this place gets hit and the priest finds us? He will tell the Nazis and they will take us to… Where would they take us? None ever tells us that.

This is the worst airraid I have ever been in and we weren't even hit.

In retrospect I realize that our fear was not of bombs or fire, or even the unknown Nazi threat. It was of being all alone, deserted. Our fear, and our shame… was of being different. No let's be honest, we were ashamed of being Jewish. We all shared that feeling. Oh, we never verbalized it to the adults in our lives. We knew they risked a lot for having us with them. We all made the promises that we would always remember and have pride in our heritage as was expected. But not one of us meant it. We were 10 going on 50... Not like other children, but aged beyond our years. And we knew that if we were not Jewish, we would not have to hide and be afraid all the time. So what is there to be proud of? It took many years before we could say "I am Jewish" without cringing.

IT'S NOT FUN

Guess being an airraid warden is absolutely no fun. I thought now that Eric is one too, we could really have a ball. Maybe play some tricks on Frau H. Eric is not Jewish but he is nice to me and so is his mother and father. Of course he is a lot older than me. Like 15 already.

So last night we went through the house after the all clear shooting to check for fires, etc. We were all the way up in the attic when bombs started falling again without any warning shots. I tried to run down to the cellar, but Eric tackled me and held me on the floor. I was never, ever so scared in my life. The frames from the windows fell in and part of the roof flew away from some explosion. Eric told me not to be afraid. That any bomb and explosion you hear is already past. But he was shaking too and besides, what about the one we don't hear? And now part of the wall fell down and some of the pieces are on top of us. Not big ones, but I am so scared. I don't know how long the raid lasted, but I think it had to be many hours... (Of course, it only seemed like that, actually it was only about 20 minutes.) After all was quiet we got up and we heard Dad and Eric's Mom yelling for us. Guess they were just as scared as we were and the rest of the people in the cellar had to block them from opening the steel doors. There are about 90 people in our cellar now, so they couldn't take a chance for two kids.

Everyone was happy to see we were alive with only some scratches and dust on us. Even Frau H. smiled at me. Mom was just waking up from a faint. She seems to faint a lot when she gets real scared. The girls look like they were crying, but all they said was "Glad to see you didn't get hurt up there."

I hope we never have to be going through the house when there are more bombs coming down. Eric said I was a brave little girl and winked at me. I am glad he didn't tell anyone how I was crying, and screaming and shaking up there. But I think he was my hero for holding me the whole time.

NO MORE HOME

Well, we finally got it last night. Our apartment is finished. And the next two floors down are also burned out. There were so many fires in the building and without water, we couldn't do too much. Somehow, the lower part of the building is fine. So we have to double up even more. There are now more than 100 people in this building and only 2 apartments left. And of course the basement and cellar. That means we sleep wall to wall or in the cellar even without an airraid. And without running water, the bathrooms are a real problem. I think the adults sneak into the ruins lots of time but I am not sure. Cooking the potatoes is hard too. It takes so much wood to have enough fire for at least 10 big pots every morning. But that is the only food we still have so we just have to find more wood. And that is getting hard too, since we cannot take it from any bombed out buildings because it is needed for the war effort. (We take it anyway, but mostly after dark and it is kind of dangerous, since you cannot see where you are stepping.)

If Dad is right and we live through this war, I will never eat another boiled potato or any kind of potato. And I will find a way to get Mom some chocolate and some coffee. She is forever talking about that. Must be some big deal for her. I would just like some hot bread from the bakery and some Schlagsahne(whipped cream). But we probably will all be dead before the war is over.

Last night the radio said that the Americans are coming and the French and the English. I do not believe this. And now we probably won't be able to listen any more since we have no place to go and hide.

NO MORE SCHOOL

So now I cannnot go to school any longer. It was real bad to-day. We had assembly and one other kid, a boy, and I were the only ones not in uniform. The principal called us up front and then told everyone there that we were Jews and had no business being in the same school with them. He said we were dirty, stupid and looked likes apes. And most of the kids cheered. Then they sang the Horst Wessel song, which is the Nazi anthem. Some of the teachers had tears in their eyes. And the boy and I were told to get out now and never come back.

I ran all the way home. And I took off all my clothes and stood in front of Mom's tall mirror. I wanted to check again if I looked any different than before. I had done this when I could not get in the Bundes Maedel. But nothing has changed. I do not have a tail. Or anything else that is different. Mom cries and I am sure the girls will do the same when they get home. But I will not cry. And I will not pray either, because it does no good. If there really was a God, he would not let this happen to me.

I wonder who the boy was and if I will ever see him again. Hope he is ok.

When Dad came home I told him what had happened. He got very upset and said that I would be better educated than any of those little Nazis out there. Yeah, right. Can't go to school, can't march, can't get a ration card. And I am going to be smarter than the rest of them? How will that happen? But Dad is so sure, and I do not want to hurt his feelings. But I don't believe him either.[1]

---

[1] I never did see the boy again and assume they probably caught him. And Dad did see to it that I was better educated than any of the other kids.

PILOTS

I have been wondering about something. Yesterday Dad brought these two men home with him.

They are very dirty and smell. And they don't even speak German. Dad brought out the Bible (as usual) to make everyone swear not to tell. Mom gave them potatoes and some peppermint tea and then they went into Dad's study. When I asked who they were, I was told it was not for me to know and to just remember I swore not to tell anyone that they were here.

And then the shooting started. That means that there are planes coming. We don't have sirens anymore, they are all bombed out. Something to do with electricity. We all went in the cellar, well actually not all of us. The two dirty men stayed in the apartment, even when the air raid started. I tried to tell Dad they might get hurt, but he shushed me and said not to worry. When the air raid was over and we came back upstairs, the men were gone. I wonder who they were and where they went. (After the war I found out they were English pilots who had been shot down and were trying to get to Switzerland and then back to England. Dad and the Lutheran Minister were trying to help them. I don't know what that man didn't do during the war to help others...)

POTATOES

Did I ever mention that Mom is a seamstress? She makes clothes for the ballet and the Opera House. And of course she makes all my clothes too and once in a while I get to try on some of the ballet costumes. What is this got to do with potatoes? You'll see in a minute.

Mom was kind of sick yesterday and she was in bed all day. Until five that is. Then she told me to get her coat and said she had to go downstairs before it got dark. I could not understand that. She goes downstairs every afternoon when it gets dark and watches the Russian ladies (they are prisoners that have to make little rocks out of big chunks of cement left after the air raids). People stare at these ladies and call them names and make fun of them. Dad says they did nothing wrong and some of them have families in

52

Russia and kids, and everything. They are treated real bad, kind of like us Jews, I guess.

Anyway, I don't understand why Mom goes and stands under the door and stares at them. She doesn't talk to them or anything. After I got her coat, Mom told me to swear never to tell what I was about to find out. And to get the Bible to swear on. That was really strange, since only Dad ever did that. Then she told me to get 14 boiled potatoes out of the big pot in the kitchen. We boiled a pot of potatoes every morning and if we got hungry, we would go and eat a potato.

When I brought the potatoes, Mom turned her coat inside out and there were all these pockets on the inside. She told me to put a potato in each pocket and then turn the coat around and help her put it on. Then she said, "I don't feel too good, so you have to go downstairs with me and help me." Help with what???? And that's when I found out that Mom was as much of a hero as Dad. She gave each of the Russian ladies a boiled potato as they walked by, and yesterday I got to do it too. And even though no one has told me so, I know it's against the law to feed these ladies or help them in any way. And I know we could get shot doing this. But I guess my family does not care about that. They keep taking all these chances for me, so I guess doing it for other people too isn't that strange.

RATION CARDS

It's ration card day. And so we go shopping. Mom gets all the bread for the week. And the meat. When we get home, she takes her baking scale and then she divides the bread into 5 pieces. We only get 4 ration cards, since I am a non-person. So the rest of the family shares their rations with me. The meat she leaves in one piece. She will cook it and then make soup with potatoes and carrots. But we all get our bread for the week.

Did I mention we all have rucksacks (backpacks) all packed with one set of clean clothes, toothbrush, comb etc. We keep those with us all the time in case of airraids. So Mom gives us our bread to put in the rucksacks and tells us again it must last all week. Mine never does, and I usually end up getting most of Dad's and Irma's. Sometimes one of the nice neighbors will give Mom some of their bread for me.

Of course we do have lots of boiled potatoes. Everyone in the building boils a big pot of potatoes each morning. And so if you get real hungry, you eat a potato. Sometimes we leave the skin on to get a different taste. But I am still hungry all the time. I hear Mom talking about what she wouldn't do for a cup of real coffee or a piece of chocolate. If we live through this war, I am going to buy her the biggest chocolate bar in the world and a big bag of real coffee. But I really don't think it will happen. We will most likely die in an airraid or the Nazis will get me.

ROBERT

Robert had a lot of bruises on him to-day. At first he wouldn't tell me who beat him up. But I kept after him and he finally told me. (Robert is my boyfriend and two years older than me). Seems somebody told Mr. B. Robert's dad, that he was always hanging around with that little Jewish kid up the street. Mr. B. is a brown shirt (SA) and holds some rank as an officer. I don't know how high up he is. Anyway, Robert had been forbidden by his Dad to go anywhere near any Jewish kids, especially the ten year old girl who was kicked out of school. That, of course, was me.

Robert had never told me about it and still came around to play or study or go for an errand with me every day. So when his dad found out, he got a real beating, Nazi style. Guess his dad knew how to do that. I told Dad what had happened, and he in turn talked to Robert and told him it

57

would be better if he stayed away from me. He told him he was afraid Robert's dad would turn me in. So, needless to say, Robert stayed away and so did the rest of the kids, after they heard what happened. Thus ends my first and last friendship. (After the war was over, Robert's family moved away and I never saw them again).

SAME QUESTION AGAIN...

I ASKED YOU WHEN I WAS ONLY EIGHT

WHY DO YOU HATE ME? WHY ARE YOU PUSHING
ME OUT THE SCHOOLYARD GATE?

I DON'T LOOK ANY DIFFERENT FROM THE REST
OF YOU.

WHY DO YOU KEEP CALLING ME A "DIRTY JEW?"

WHEN IT COMES TO THE '3Rs' I DO REALLY WELL;

IN FACT I WAS ALWAYS DONE LONG BEFORE THE
BELL.

Edith Rogers

MY TEACHER HE LIKED ME, HE HAD TEARS IN HIS
EYES,

THE NAZIS TOOK HIM AWAY, EVENTUALLY TOOK
HIS LIFE.

DID HE COMMIT A HORRIBLE CRIME? NO…

JUST FORGED MY FAMILY TREE TO BUY ME SOME
TIME.

SOME TIME TO LIVE, TO LEARN, TO GROW.

HE DID NOT BELIEVE A JEW MUST FOREGO

THE DIGNITIES A GOOD LIFE SHOULD BRING.

I KEPT ON ASKING, "WHAT IS THIS THING CALLED A JEW?"

NO ONE EVER ANSWERED MY QUESTION.

WHY DIDN'T YOU??

MS. SIMON

It was way past time for breakfast. Ms. Simon, our maid, had not come down from her room in the attic of the building. So Dad sent me to fetch her. Her room was unlocked, but she was not there. I wandered around the area in the attic where kids were not supposed to be. Guess because of the unfinished areas where a kid could fall in. Anyway, I went there and I found Ms. Simon. She was hanging from one of the beams and swaying back and forth. I told her it was time for breakfast and to come down right now. Deep inside I probably knew she was dead but could not face it. So I went downstairs and told Mom and Dad what I found. Mom promptly fainted and Dad ran upstairs. It seems strange, but no one ever told me anything other than that Ms. Simon went away. After all, I was only a kid. (Or so the adults thought.) They never realized that I was never just a child. The Nazis stole my childhood from me and I have never forgiven them for that.

SOUPKITCHEN

There is a soupkitchen at the old schoolbuilding. Each family can come and get a pot of soup as long as they have a ration card receipt. It's a long walk and we decided to take a little wagon. Some of the neighbors asked if I could go get their soup and in return they would share some with me. Dad said ok and so I go to the school with the wagon and 9 souppots and the rationcard receipts. Of course Mrs. H. is going to get her own. She is probably afraid I would poison the soup, and you know what? I would if I could. Told Dad and he said that would make me as bad as her. Yeah, right… Wish I could at least do something to her and those two snotty kids, R and E.

Anyway, we got soup. It even has meat in it. Everyone says that it is horsemeat. But who cares? It tastes good and we just hope the kitchen stays open a long time. I will go every day for our building if I can.

We also have a waterwagon coming every day. We get only so much water, but it's ok. It's better than nothing. And Mom and Mrs. B. made some candles out of something, so we even have some lights some of the time.

To-morrow Dad and Erik and I are going to find wood for heat. Noone has any coal left and of course we have no gas. So we need wood to cook and heat. We will first go to the forests and then maybe some of the bombed out buildings. We take the wagon and load it. Everyone in the building will get their turn. Even Mrs. H. as long as she does not turn me in. I heard Dad tell Mom(eavesdropping again) that Mrs. H will never turn me in, because her husband has forbidden it. That's strange, since he never ever talks to me when I see him. He works for the railroad

65

and Dad says he knows about a lot of things that he can't talk about. But he is one of the good guys. Well, if Dad says so.

STEALING?

Last night was Eric's and my turn to go out and get food during the airraid alarm. We were real lucky because no bombs fell and no one caught us either.

Let me explain this. Every time there is an alarm, two people from our building go out and get food. They have to be from two different families to keep everyone from telling. We go and get things like potatoes, apples, carrots, cabbages, cucumbers, etc.

We get these by the basket full. We only dig them up or take them from trees in the Nazi farms. Never from regular people that have a little garden or something.

You could call it stealing, but we don't think so. It means that everyone in our building will be able to have some food. There are now almost a hundred people here, since our building is the only one still standing on the block. Even with the food coupons we cannot get any food. There is a soupwagon every two days. And of course the water wagon comes by every morning. Did I mention we have not had any water, gas or electricity for a couple of months now? Each family gets two pails of water per day. And our families still make us wash every day. Sometimes we could just stay dirty, couldn't we. But oh no, we have to scrub our elbows and wash our ears.

I am going off the track here. I was telling you about getting the food. Anyway, we climb over the fence and we take turns acting as the looker. To make sure no one is coming. But the Nazi guards are in the shelters, that's why we only go during the alarms.

So last night we got a big sack of potatoes and a basket full of carrots. Mom and the other ladies will boil the potatoes and clean the carrots. Those are real good to chew on when you get hungry.

Do you think we are thieves? We do not steal from our neighbors and we share with everyone.

Even take some to the sisters.

Edith Rogers

THE DENTIST

A strange thing happened last night. Dr. B., the dentist next door, was bombed out. He is the one who always calls Dad when it is time to take me to the Sisters. Guess he knows about things, because he is a big Nazi, a Gauleiter and BrownShirt. But Dad had me swear on the Bible not to tell anyone that Dr. B. helps to hide me. I am not sure I like that man. He never talks to me, and acts as if I was not there. Anyway, we were taking his stuff out of the burning building and Dad and I were emptying his desk drawers. A little tiny drawer fell out of the back of the desk. It had a ring, some pictures and some other papers in it. Instead of putting it in the basket we were using, Dad put it all in his pockets. I cannot believe my Dad would steal something. And after we got home, out came the Bible with the same old rigmarole, of swearing not to tell, and so on. I was so shocked, that I cried while I was swearing and that night in bed, I wondered if anything made any sense. Not my Dad. He was the most honest man, and a hero. Why would he do that?

The years have passed, the war is over. I am not too young to ask questions now. The ring was Dr. B's Mason ring, the Mason's being some outlawed organization. The pictures and other papers had something to do with the same thing and Dad realized it right away and hid it from the others.

Dad released me from my oath so I could tell the judge when Dr. B. was brought into court for being a Gauleiter. I told all I knew, including the fact that without Dr. B's. help, I would not have survived. I do not know if Dr. B. had to serve any time or anything. I hope not.

THE OLD MAN

The old man was coming up the street. He was wearing a yellow star. Some of the kids in the neighborhood, including a cousin of mine, were watching him.

As he came closer, some of the kids started picking up rocks from the bombed out buildings and throwing them at the old man and some of the kids spat at him.. My cousin, whose own mother was Jewish, though he didn't know it, was one of those kids. I had strict instructions to always come inside immediately if anything involving Jews went on, but this time I disobeyed. I grabbed my cousin and threw him on the street and started beating him up. It was the old Jewish man, with tears in his eyes, who pulled me off and said, that the child does not know any better and to leave him be. How could he feel that way?? He had to wear

72

the star and be spit at and everything. I will never understand this. I know that everytime someone refers to me as the dirty little Jewish girl, I want to beat them up…

THE SISTERS...

IT'S TIME TO GO TO THE SISTERS AGAIN,

FOR A LITTLE WHILE ONLY, YOU TELL ME.

IT IS THE MIDDLE OF THE NIGHT

I AM SLEEPY AND DO NOT WANT TO GO THERE AND HIDE.

HIDE FROM THE GESTAPO, HIDE FROM THE PRIEST TOO.

SAY PRAYERS EVERY MORNING, NOON AND EVE.

NEVER KNOWING WHEN I CAN LEAVE.

OR IF EVER I CAN GO HOME.

EACH "LITTLE WHILE ONLY" GETS LONGER AND LONGER.

EVERY DAY MY FEAR BECOMES STRONGER

THAT THIS TIME THE GESTAPO WILL KNOW WHERE I AM

THEY WILL COME AND GET ME, AND THE

THE "LITTLE WHILE ONLY" WILL BE FOREVER

AND GOING HOME WILL HAPPEN-NEVER.

THE PRAYING THE SISTERS DO WON'T HELP

I LOVE THEM ALL, THEY FEED ME, THEY HUG ME

AND KISS ME GOOD NIGHT.

THEY EVEN TEACH ME MATH AND OTHER THINGS SO I MIGHT

STILL KEEP UP MY EDUCATION.

THEY TELL ME THAT ALL THIS SOMEDAY WILL BE OVER

AND I WILL SURELY FORGET.

WELL, IT HAPPENED A LIFETIME AGO,

BUT I HAVE NOT FORGOTTEN ANY OF IT YET.

TUNNEL

We are building a tunnel from our house to the ones next door. This is in case either of the buildings get bombed and we can't get out the cellar door. So everyone is digging and filling pails and throwing the dirt in the courtyard. Don't know how they got under the cement, but somehow they did. This is actually fun. We can even plant some flowers in the dirt and maybe some tomatoes or something. The men are putting some wood in the tunnels to shore them up so they won't fall down on anyone. Since I am the smallest I get to try crawling through first. I got scared in the dark down there but I wouldn't tell anyone. And I got all the way through both tunnels.

Now it's Mom's turn, since she is the biggest. Oh, she got real angry about being the biggest. She says she is no fatter than some of the other women. But she finally agrees to try the tunnel from the right while Mrs. B. tries from the left one. Well, they both got stuck about halfway and had to back out. We kids thought it was funny. Imagine this, two heavy women crawling backwards out of a dirt tunnel! But none of the adults thought is was funny at all and I guess if the tunnel needed to be used to get out, it wouldn't be. So we all got yelled at and then had to start digging again. After about a week we are finally finished and Mom and Mrs. B had no trouble getting through. Hopefully noone will ever need to use it. We boarded all entrances up with wood but we all know how to open up if we need to.

WHAT IS A JEW?

I WENT TO JOIN THE BUNDES MAEDEL TO-DAY.

THEY WOULDN'T LET ME IN, BECAUSE I AM A 'DIRTY JEW.'

NOW I AM A VERY CLEAN GIRL SO THAT PART IS WRONG.

WHAT ABOUT THE OTHER PART? THE JEW?

WHAT DOES THAT MEAN?

AM I A JEW? AND IF SO, WHY DID THE GIRLS SAY I WOULD DISGRACE THE FLAG AND THE UNIFORM?

I WOULDN'T DO THAT.

PLEASE DAD, HELP ME TO JOIN, I WANT TO BE A
BUNDES MAEDEL.

I WANT TO WEAR A UNIFORM, I WANT TO MARCH
IN THE PARADES

AND CARRY THE FLAG.

DAD? WHY WON'T YOU ANSWER ME? AND WHY
DO YOU HAVE TEARS IN YOUR EYES? ARE YOU
ANGRY WITH ME? WHAT DID I DO?

ARE YOU ANGRY OR SAD THAT I AM A JEW?

MAYBE YOU DON'T KNOW WHAT IT MEANS
EITHER.

Edith Rogers

BUT YOU KNOW EVERYTHING, SO PLEASE TELL
ME

WHAT IS A JEW?

VISIT TO THE HOSPITAL

Now that Dad says none of the family can leave the house alone, it is no fun. The reason not one of us can even go to the store alone, is that an air raid may happen, destroy the house and then only one would survive. This has happened to a lot of Dad's friends, and he says it is better if at least two people are still together, if it should happen. So now I have to go everyplace Irma or Lotte go, or if Mom or Dad want to go someplace, one of us has to go. It is a real drag. I get so bored when Irma goes to her girlfriends' house. They talk about movie stars, and stuff like that. Yuck... At least with Lotte, I get to talk about the war and things like history, and books and stuff. She is smart, like Dad.

So yesterday, Irma had to report to the hospital where she works. There had been another air raid the night before, and it was real hard getting there. The streets were hot from the burning buildings, and there was a lot of broken walls on the street and we had to climb over some ruins. When we got to the hospital, there was a line of people laying on the ground, asleep. I asked Irma why she had to come to work, if these people were just lying there sleeping. I don't know what happened, but she started screaming, she threw herself on the ground and pounded on it. She was all out of control. I couldn't get her to stop, so I walked up to one of the sleeping people and kicked her, to get her to help me. Oh God, she was not sleeping, Her eyes were wide open and she was dead. I had just kicked a dead person. I don't get too easily shook, but I had to throw up. Irma finally got quiet and and took me by the hand and we went inside. There was not much left. Most of the inside was burned out. There were a few people still wandering around. One of the doctors said that the patients that were saved, were in the back. So we went there and helped feed them. Irma helped some of them to get dressed in some of the clothes they had saved. I mostly just sat there. I did not feel like I wanted to do anything. We were all going to die anyway, it was just a matter of time, whatever that meant. (I had heard a lot of people say that lately.)

After a while Irma was done and we started home. By then, it had started to rain, like it always did the day after an airraid. It's strange, but somehow the fires made clouds and then this dirty, black rain would come down the next day. And the smell... It was a long walk home, probably one of the worst of my life. We had to take all kinds of long way around streets to get back. I went straight to sleep when we finally got there. I did not want to talk to anyone, not even Dad.

THEY ARE COMING

It is April 21, 1945 and it may actually be over.

We can hear the artillery shooting. This means the Allied troops are coming. Dad is real excited, but some of the others are saying it will be worse. And the loudspeaker trucks just announced that all men over the age of 12 must report to the edge of town immediately. No one in our block is going except for Fritz and Eric. They are wearing their HitlerYouth uniforms and carrying their rifles. Dad and Eric's Mom and Fritz's Oma (grandmother) are trying to stop them. But they won't listen. So Dad has knocked Fritz down and is taking his gun and Eric is giving him his gun. So they are told to get out of the uniforms and get into something else. Fritz has no other clothes left and so he has to wear my long pants and one of the girl's sweater. Eric

86

has borrowed some clothes from somewhere or maybe his Oma still had some of his. I don't know. The boys from the building are hiding in the cellar behind some fake walls that we built some time ago for me but Dad says I won't need them. He says I will be save now. Could that really be true?

Irma and I are on the street and Dad almost knocked us down. Guess the little pings we heard are bullets and we are in danger. So everyone has to go in the cellar. Both Irma and Lotte have a rifle and say if the Nazis still come to get me on the last day, they will shoot them. All of a sudden there is the banging on the steel door. Dad opens it with the girls pointing their rifles at whoever it may be. Whoa, Dad lets loose with a stream of French and the girls drop their rifles and run and hug the soldiers standing there.

87

I do not know what Dad said, but the officer picks me up and hugs and kisses me and everyone, even Frau H. is crying. I guess it really is over.

I wonder if Mutti is coming home with Peter and if I will see some of my friends like Guido or Mr. Haug.

For now the war is over for us. The French officer puts a French flag on what is left of our building. He says it will keep us save from looters and soldiers that are not nice. And we get some stuff to eat. It's from some kind of tin can and tastes pretty good. And Dad and Eric and some of the older women all have a drink of some kind with the officer and toast each other and the French officer kisses everyone on each cheek.

But down the street we hear some shooting going on. One of the Hitler Youth from another block is shooting at the soldiers. They don't know he is only 14 and they kill him. Fritz and Eric are very upset, because they think they did not do their duty by not going out and defending the block like they were supposed to. It takes all the adults to calm them down and tell them they could not have stopped the tanks parked down the block or the armored cars or even the soldiers on foot. The war is over and the Germans lost.

This makes some of the people very sad and some upset. But they are also glad that there will be no more airraids and maybe we will get water and food and even lights and gas back when the rebuilding starts. And Dad says it will start sooner than we think. And I said before, he knows everything, so he must be right.

Well, the war is over. I am no longer a mixling 1st degree. Strange, since I am the same person I was yesterday. So what has changed? I still have a Jewish mother, wherever she may be. Oh yes, the Nazis are not in power anymore. Will that make it all ok? Will the bad times be forgotten? I do not think so.

Will I be able to forget the constant fear I have been in for years?

What happened to all the people that were "relocated" during the war. My mother and Peter? Of course, I only saw Peter once and do not really miss him. But I do miss my mother, whom I have not seen in years. I used to see her at least 4 or 5 times a year before all this stuff started. Now I don't know if she is even alive.

Dad says I can now get rid of the star on my coat in the closet. He says I will never have to worry about it again. I don't really believe that, but I don't tell him that.

It is real easy to forget things that happened, or so I am told. However, I cannot forget the two mentally retarded kids who were killed by exhaust from a big car. They didn't hurt anybody. In fact, they were always smiling and sweet.

Dad says we won't need ration cards any more. Great, except there is no food in the stores anyway. We are still eating mostly potatoes. But Dad says it will get better very soon. Hope he is right. All Mom talks about is wanting a good cup of coffee. Maybe she will get one soon. I would like some good fresh bread and some whipped cream. One can dream for those things. And we do not have any more air raids. That is great. No more hiding out with the Sisters either. Dad took me over there yesterday, mostly to say thank you for helping us out. I guess I am the only one of the five of us still in town. Noone knows where the other four kids are. Maybe they will come back now that it is all over. Dad and the Sisters had tears when they talked about it all. It does not look too good for the other four.

Dad is talking again about how I should go to the USA when I grow up. Sure... In the meantime, I will continue to learn English. I also try a little French and Russian, but I am getting too confused so I will just stick to English. And I will try and make up for all the good things the family did for me. I still don't understand most of what went on, but every day more horrible things are told to us.

They say that all the people that were relocated are dead. That most of them were tortured and killed with gas. It is probably just rumors. Even the Nazis could not have killed that many people, could they?

Forget what I just said. Going to the trains coming back from the camps changed my mind. Those people look like zombies. They are too skinny and weak to walk and they have that awful look in their eyes. It scares me and I will have nightmares, I bet. Dad says that those are just a "few" of the ones they (the Nazis) took away. And that most of the rumors are true.

Dad also tells me I should now try and remember the good times I sometimes had. Like going to his office with him and learning how to type there. And letting me be the office cleaning lady. Of course, he didn't mention that the office burnt down in an air raid.

And the long Sunday morning walks I took with him. Those were real fun. We picked flowers and wild strawberrys. And sometimes we would visit some of his friends and I would get to listen to them talk about the good old days.

I better not forget that Mom used to take me to the opera house with her and I got to see a lot of rehearsals for the ballet and the opera. And since I was little, sometimes she would use me to try on the ballet costumes to make changes.

We went to a museum that was open yesterday. And there were no pictures of Hitler, no flags and noone playing or singing the usual songs. That was a surprise, but Dad says it is going to be that way from now on. Could he be right? I don't know. I am still a little scared but not as much as I used to be.

We can listen to any radio station we want to now. No more Nazi songs are on. I like the music we hear a lot. The girls tell me that they are all old tunes, but probably new ones will soon come out. And some of the tunes are American. So, things are really changing. And the bad times are almost gone.

PS: I did eventually come to the USA. I became a citizen. Other than the birth of my children/grandchildren, the happiest day of my life was when I took my Oath of Allegiance to the United States of America. The German government had offered to give me my citizenship back before I left Germany, but I very impolitely declined. I have never gone back to Europe. I never did get a definitive date of the death of my mother or brother, only that they went to Theresienstadt and then to Auschwitz. There the trail ends.

Peter

Mutti

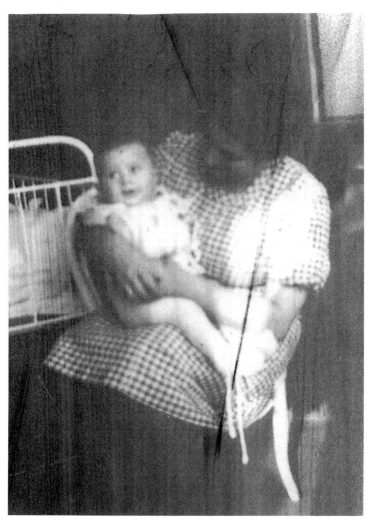

Mutti and Peter

Irma   **Mom**   **Lotte**

Mutti

Mom

Dad

ABOUT THE AUTHOR

The author, Edith C. Rogers, was born in Saarbruecken, Germany in the early 1930s. When she was two years old, she was sent on a visit to her great aunt in Stuttgart, Germany. This visit was to be for a few weeks, but she remained for the next twenty years.

When the first race laws regarding inter-marriage with Jews were passed, her father divorced her mother and abandoned her.

Considering the political climate in Germany, staying in Stuttgart was thought to be best for the little girl. While no one ever could have imagined what was in store for the Jews in Germany, this without doubt saved the author's life. While no official papers for guardianship or adoption were ever filed, the author came to think of the family in Stuttgart as her own and even used their name sometimes.

The author has four *children,* ten grandchildren and two great-grand children. She is currently enjoying retirement and living in the Chicago, Illinois area.

Made in the USA
Lexington, KY
21 November 2016